A Whaling Captain's Life

A Whaling Captain's Life

The Exciting True Account by Henry Acton for His Son, William

ILLUSTRATED WITH 112 PLATES

Charleston · London

History
PRESS

COLLECTOR'S EDITION OF
THE 1838 NEW ENGLAND CLASSIC

Published by The History Press
Charleston, SC 29403
www.historypress.net

Originally published 1838
The History Press edition 2008

Manufactured in the United Kingdom

ISBN 978.1.59629.417.2

Library of Congress CIP data applied for.

From the Publisher:
This new edition contains the full text from the original 1838 edition, published by Ives and Jewett. Original material used in the production of this book from the collection of Gus Sousa, former interim director of the Salem Anthenaeum.

Notice: The information in this book is true and complete to the best of our knowledge. It is offered without guarantee on the part of the author or The History Press. The author and The History Press disclaim all liability in connection with the use of this book.

DANGERS OF THE WHALE FISHERY.

This delightful little book from 1838 takes us back to a time when neither whale nor seal hunting was judged but for its bounty. It was, then, a normal employment, a way of life that brought with it high risk, possibly high reward and, always, an adrenaline-rushing adventure for the men with the courage to pursue it.

The charm of this book is that it is delivered from a father to his son with honesty and integrity. There are no descriptions puffed with drama.

Whether Henry is describing the realities of a hunt in stormy seas, or a ship being flung into midair by the flip of an angry, threatened whale, he does so with an earnest tone.

This is all about a father teaching his son about the way the world worked for the hunters and the hunted, and the plain facts of what practical purposes these animals served once they met their demise. This is the kind of adventure story any father would engage in with his son to help him understand life, the magnificence of nature and how the fibers of each connect in survival.

Henry sets the stage for his story with a natural history of the whale—"the mightiest animals that swim the ocean stream." We learn from him, through his personal experiences with the creatures at sea, how they live, what they eat, their relationships with their young and the secrets of their bodies—"the tail is the most active limb of this mighty animal...a single blow throws a large boat with its crew into the air."

We learn too the most sought-after of their species and the products they provide to the men who take them down. We learn they have no voice except for the haunting sounds from the blowhole, they are "dull of hearing" and their vision is poor. It is apparent in Henry's storytelling that this information comes from the hunters' continued study of the creatures, likely after hundreds of trips to sea as they strategized for a successful kill. Henry shares with his son how these gentle sea giants can be taken from behind when the light, quick boats, armed with men and harpoons, are never seen or heard. Experience has taught them where to pierce for success.

In the chapter "The Taking of a Whale with Her Young," the mothers and their young are noted as easy targets. Where they travel, they are stalked. And it is the young whale that in effect becomes a sea-bound marker for the mother and her eventual fate as she tries to protect her youngster.

Soon we learn the details of the boats—what makes them so swift in the chase, and what equipment is used to stalk and eventually kill the whale. It all starts with the officer, perched in his crow's-nest—a fragile little sentry box—his spyglass pointed to the open ocean. The sight of a whale would likely send a cry that thundered across the boat, "Whale ahead!"

Is it early morning; is it dusk? Are the seas rough and stormy or as calm as silk? Is there a chill in the air as the men tumble into the boats and rush, cracking their oars into the water, moving closer and closer to the whale's back? And we can't help but think what those moments might have been like when a young man saw the tail begin to soar and lift his boat to the blue sky—when he knew this was the moment that bridged life and death for him, and for the whale.

But by this chapter, we know a little about the whale, too, and the contrast of this innocent giant being readied for death touches our core.

When Henry shares the stories of whales that have pulled their way free and in their battle for life killed men and sent boats to the bottom of the sea, we can ponder life's lessons.

In "Proceedings After a Whale Is Killed," the author brings us along for the after-hunt surgeries that transform the animal into half-ton, portable cubes or oblong pieces of blubber, a whalebone and jawbone. The carcass is turned to the sea, and the floating scraps of flesh become a meal for a flock of gulls.

In the chapter "Catching Seal," Henry brings his son and us an equally compelling story of the species, how they live, how they are hunted, the dangers the hunters face and what products the seals bring man.

It is easy to imagine this book being read to Henry's dear son William—from a father who does not want to be forgotten, who wants his son to take in the simple truths of life, whether of the hunter or the hunted.

If you have ever wondered what this life was like, here you have a story from a captain who lived it—spoken honestly—bringing a chapter of history to a uniquely personal level. Settle in to your favorite reading chair, and join Captain

Henry Acton as he takes you on long-forgotten adventures of a time when life was simple and the journey always complex.

The Editors at The History Press

CATCHING

OF THE

WHALE AND SEAL;

OR,

HENRY ACTON'S CONVERSATION TO HIS SON WILLIAM

ON THE

𝔚𝔥𝔞𝔩𝔢 𝔞𝔫𝔡 𝔖𝔢𝔞𝔩 𝔉𝔦𝔰𝔥𝔢𝔯𝔶.

WITH PLATES.

𝔖𝔞𝔩𝔢𝔪:

PUBLISHED BY IVES AND JEWETT.

NEW YORK: GOULD AND NEWMAN.

1838.

CONTENTS.

NATURAL HISTORY OF THE WHALE.

CHAPTER I.

THE DIFFERENT AND MOST REMARKABLE SPECIES OF THE WHALE TRIBE.

" Nature's strange work, vast Whales of different form,
Toss up the troubled flood, and are themselves a storm.
Uncouth the sight, when they, in dreadful play,
Discharge their nostrils, and refund a sea."

You recollect, my son, that some time since in a morning's walk you pointed out to me an enormous arch over a field gate, which I told you was formed of the jaw-bones of the whale, and I then promised you an account of these enormous fishes. Among the num-

berless tribes of living animals that people
the northern seas, the class of whales are by
far the largest, and although living in the
water, they are in many respects similar to
quadrupeds; they not only bring forth their
young alive, but suckle them as do the land
animals; they have also a thick layer of fatty
substance, called blubber, surrounding their
whole body, beneath the skin, and it is by
this covering, my son, that Providence ena-
bles them to defy the most dreadful extrem-
ities of cold even under the ice at the Poles.
Although they are the "mightiest animals
that swim the ocean stream" their bulk has
been often exaggerated, they being rarely
more than 60 feet long, which implies a
weight of 70 tons, being nearly that of 300

fat oxen. The tail is the most active limb of this mighty animal; its power is tremendous; a single blow throws a large boat with its crew into the air. There are several varieties of the whale. The most dangerous one is the Razor Back, which is longer than the Common Black or Right Whale, and although smaller in circumference, is a more powerful animal, swimming at the rate of twelve miles an hour, and has been known to run off 480 fathoms of line with a harpoon attached to him in one minute. They are difficult to obtain, often obliging the sailors to cut the line in order to escape destruction; but as this species contains only ten or twelve tons of oil of an inferior quality, the whalers generally shun his encounter; sometimes however they mistake him in the water for the common one. The other species of whale eagerly sought after by man, is the Cachalot or Spermaceti; this animal is almost invariably found in large herds of from 150 to 200.

CHAPTER II.

THE Spermaceti as well as the Common Whale feeds on the smallest insects or animalcula of the ocean, its capacious mouth with the vast fringes of whalebone attached to the inside of its mouth is a most excellent filter, enabling it to receive a large quantity of water at a mouthful, and to separate the sea-weed and gravel from it, even of the size of a pin's head. This substance, called whalebone, is taken from the upper jaw of the animal, and is very different from the real bones, which resemble those of great land animals. When we reflect, my son, that the same *almighty power*, whose will has formed the immense whale, has also given animation and senses to the smallest sea insects which are the food of this marine monster, how must our pride be lowered, while we are so unable to comprehend the mechanism which puts them in motion, and much less that intelligence and power which has given them life. Let us then exclaim in astonishment and gratitude with the sweet singer of Israel, " O Lord, how inscrutable are thy ways, how magnificent thy works !" As the whale must rise to the surface of the sea to breathe, its tail is placed horizontally, to enable it to ascend and descend more quickly. This animal is dull of hearing, although its sense of seeing is acute. They will discover one another in clear water when under the surface at an amazing distance; when at the top of the water however they do not see far. They have no voice, but in breathing or blowing they make a very loud noise; they throw the water through their blow holes, which are situated upon the head, many yards high, which looks at a distance like a puff of smoke; and, when the whale is wounded, is often red with blood. Although this animal is so large, it will sometimes descend perpendicularly after being harpooned, at the astonishing velocity of eight miles an hour; their usual rate of swimming when not pursued is never more than half that number. They are seldom found asleep; they are however *occa-*

sionally found sleeping in calm weather among the ice in northern latitudes. When the whale feeds, it swims pretty swiftly with its mouth open just below the surface of the sea. This animal has but one young at a time, which is from ten to fifteen feet long at its birth; it goes with its mother for at least one year, until it is supposed that the whalebone or filter has grown sufficient to enable it to procure its own food. The love of the whale for its young is great, so that whalers, whenever they can harpoon them, are pretty sure of getting its parent; for whenever the young rises to the surface of the water to breathe, the old whale will join and encourage it to swim off, and will often take it under her fin, and seldom deserts it

while life remains. I will give you, William, to-morrow, an incident which took
place in 1811, on board of a Northern Whaler.

CHAPTER III.

In the spring of 1811, on board of Capt.
Scoresby's ship, one of the harpooners
struck a young whale, with the hope of its
leading to the capture of its mother. Presently she arose close by his boat and seizing its young one dragged out nearly 100
fathoms of line with amazing swiftness.
Again she arose to the surface, darted furiously on and appeared in great agony, seemingly regardless of the danger which surrounded her. At length one of the boats
came near enough to throw a harpoon which

hit, but did not hold; a second harpoon fail-
ed also, but the third was fastened; still she
did not attempt to escape, but allowed other boats to approach so that in a few minutes three more harpoons were fastened,
and in the course of an hour afterwards she
was killed. Is it not extremely painful,
William, to destroy an animal of so much
affection for its young? There are also two
enemies to the whale found in the sea, the
Sword Fish and a cetaceous animal called
by our fishermen the Killer. At the sight
of the former the whale seems agitated in
an extraordinary manner, leaping from the
water as if with affright; wherever it appears, the whale perceives it at a distance,
and flies from it in an opposite direction,

2

and having no instrument of defence except
its tail, it endeavors to strike it; but the
Sword Fish is as active as the other is strong,
and easily eludes the blow. It often cuts
the whale in such a manner as to colour the
water all around with blood. The Killer is
a more destructive enemy, with strong and
very powerful teeth. A number of these
fish are said to surround the whale, some at-
tacking it with their teeth behind, others
before, till at last he dies from the loss of
blood; and what is singular, my son, it is said
that the tongue of the whale is the only part
they devour. The whale is naturally a timid animal, for it is said that the Northern
Petrel, a bird of the genus of the Mother
Cary's Chicken of our coasts, will some-

times alight upon its back, and set it off in great agitation and terror. It is also frequently annoyed by the larger species of Sharks, as the wounds sometimes found upon their tails evidently show. The flesh of the whale is highly prized by the Esquimaux, who not only eat the very fattest part, but will drink the oil with great relish; the children, also, devour the skin raw. Capt. Lyon, who was present at a feast in an Esquimaux village, says: "the houses were all lighted up with lamps, all the pots were filled with flesh, and the women, while cooking, pick out and devour the most dainty morsels. One man takes up a large piece, applies it to his mouth, and severs with his teeth as much as his mouth can possibly hold, then hands it to his neighbor, and he passes it to the next, till all is eaten; a new piece is then supplied, and thus it continues till they are completely gorged. A young man named Toolooak received into his stomach in 21 hours upwards of ten pounds of flesh and a gallon and a pint of water." The obtaining of their food is so precarious, my son, that for many days after this they may not have a single morsel to eat.

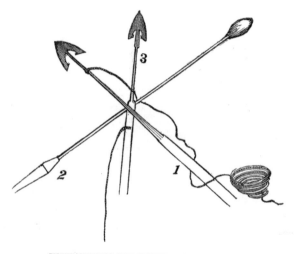

INSTRUMENTS FOR TAKING THE WHALE.

No. 1. Hand Harpoon.　　No. 2. Blubber Lance.　　No. 3. Gun Harpoon.

CHAPTER IV.

BOATS — HAND HARPOON—BLUBBER LANCE—GUN HARPOON
—MANNER OF TAKING THE WHALE, &c.

———

> " As when enclosing harpooneers assail,
> In *wintry* seas, the slumbering Whale ;
> Soon as the *harpoons* pierce the scaly side,
> He groans, he darts impetuous down the tide ;
> And rack'd all o'er with lacerating pain,
> He flies remote beneath the flood in vain."

———

THE first and principal thing, my son, in the whaling ships, are the boats, which are made to float lightly upon the water; their bow and stern are made sharp, and they are capable of being rowed with great speed, and readily turned round, — and are of such size as to carry six or seven men and seven or eight hundred weight of whale-lines. The instruments used in the capture

are the harpoon and lance ; besides these
they have used occasionally the harpoon-gun,
which is a kind of swivel. This gun was
invented in the year 1731 : being however
difficult and somewhat dangerous in its ap-
plication, it is now seldom used. One of
the most essential particulars in the Dutch
whale ships is the " *Crow's Nest,*" a sort of
sentry box made of canvass or light wood,
pitched on the main-top-mast head. This
is the post of honor, where the master or
officer of the watch often sits for hours provided with a spy glass, a speaking trumpet,
and a rifle gun. As soon as they have arrived in those seas which are the haunt of the
whale, the crew are keeping watch day and
night ;—seven boats are kept hanging by
the sides of the ship ready to be launched
in a few minutes. The captain or some

principal officer, seated in the crow's nest,
surveys the waters, and the instant he sees
the back of the huge animal, gives notice to
the watch who are stationed upon the deck,
part of whom leap into the boat, and are followed by a second boat, a harpooner being
in each. Owing to those mighty fields and
mountains of ice, the dangers of the Northern or Greenland whale fishery is ten times
greater than are those of this country, as our
whale ships take these fish upon the coast
of Japan, in the Pacific Ocean, and upon the
Brazil Banks, and always in the open sea.
There are several rules among whalers
which are observed in approaching this fish,
to prevent as far as possible the animal from
taking the alarm. As the whale is dull of
hearing, but quick in sight, the boat steerer
always endeavors to get behind it. Smooth,

careful rowing is always requisite, and sometimes sculling is practised. Whenever a
whale lies on the surface of the water, un-
conscious of the approach of its enemies,
the hardy fisher rows directly upon it; and
an instant before the boat touches it, buries
his harpoon in its back: the wounded whale,
in the surprise and agony of the moment,
makes a convulsive effort to escape; then,
my dear son, is the moment of danger. The
boat is subjected to the most violent blows
from its head or its fins, but particularly from
its ponderous tail, which sometimes sweeps
the air with such tremendous fury, that both
boat and men are exposed to one common
destruction. The head of the whale is
avoided, because it cannot be penetrated
with the harpoon; but any part of the body
between the head and tail, will admit of the

CATCHING WHALE IN THE ARCTIC SEAS.

full length of the instrument. The utmost
care is necessary in every person in the
boat, while the lines are running out—fatal
consequences having sometimes arisen from
the entanglement of the line while the whale
is going with amazing swiftness. A sailor
from Greenock, in 1818, happening to step
into the centre of a coil of running rope, had
his foot entirely carried off; another belonging to the ship Henrietta had carelessly cast
some part of the line under his feet, when a
sudden dart of the fish made it twist round
his body, and he had but just time to cry
out, "Clear away the line! O dear!" when
he was cut almost asunder, dragged over-
board and never more seen. The immense
distances to which whales will run is very
surprising; a harpoon was thrown from the
boat of the ship Resolution, in 1812, into

one, which run out 10,440 yards, or about six miles of line.

Every boat fast to a living whale carries a flag, and the ships to which such boats belong, also wear a flag, until the whale is either killed or makes its escape. These signals serve to indicate to surrounding ships the exclusive title of the "fast ship" to the entangled whale, and to prevent their interference, excepting in the way of assistance in the capture. A full grown whale generally occupies the whole of the boats belonging to one ship in its capture, which sometimes takes the whole day; they have been taken in half an hour from the throwing of the harpoon. The ease with which some whales are killed, is truly surprising; but with others it is equally astonishing that neither line nor harpoon can effect their capture. Some escape with four or five harpoons, while others equally large have been killed with a single harpoon; indeed, my son, whales have been taken by the entanglement of a line, without any harpoon at all. One was taken by the crew of the ship Nautilus, in 1814, by its accidentally having taken the line into its mouth, and by the compression of its lips, they having cut the end of the line from a whale which they had just killed; and as it was sinking in the water, another one engaged in feeding was advancing with its mouth wide open, accidentally caught this line between its extended jaws, which induced it to shut its mouth and grasp the line so firmly as to effect its capture.

A whale sometimes causes danger by proving to be alive after having exhibited

every symptom of death. Capt. Scoresby
mentions the instance of one which appeared so decidedly dead, that he himself had
leaped on the tail, and was putting a rope
through it, when he suddenly felt him sinking from beneath him. He made a spring
towards a boat that was some yards distant,
and grasping its side was drawn on board.
The fish then moved forwards, reared his
tail aloft, and shook it with such prodigious
violence, that it could have been heard for
several miles off. After a few minutes of
this violent struggle he rolled on his side and
expired.

The many accidents which have taken
place in the Greenland and Spitzbergen
whale fishery, even under the direction of the
most experienced mariners are lamentable
and manifold; and I will now, William, re-

late to you some of the many which have
occurred to the English and Dutch whalers.
The most common is that of a ship being
beset and sometimes dashed to pieces by
the collision of those mighty masses or mountains of ice with which northern seas are
continually filled. The Blecker, Capt. Pitt,
was driven against the ice with such violence that in an instant all her rigging was
dashed in pieces; the crew, however, escaped upon the ice, and after a few days were
taken off by a Dutch ship. Capt. Bile, some
years afterwards, lost a ship richly laden,
which went down suddenly; after which
the crew wandered in boats over the sea for
fourteen days before they were taken up.
Thirteen other vessels perished the same
year in those seas. Three years afterwards,
Capt. Bile lost a second ship, the crew hav-

ing just time to save themselves on the ice.

William here asked his father if whale ships were not sometimes lost at sea? Yes, my son, many fishing-ships as well as merchantmen have foundered at sea, and have never been heard from since their departure. I remember, father, says William, a **piece of poetry** which aunt Mary learnt me a long time since on the loss of a vessel.

> Deep in the silent waters,
> A thousand fathoms low,
> A stately ship lies perishing,
> She foundered long ago.

> There were blessings poured upon her,
> When from her port she sailed,
> And prayers and anxious weeping,
> Went with her o'er the sea.

> But how that fine ship perished,
> None knew, save him on high;
> No island heard her signal,
> No other bark was nigh.

We only know from Boston
She sailed, far o'er the main ;
We only know to Boston
She never came again.

You will find, my son, by referring to Irving's Sketch Book, a most thrilling description of a wreck at sea.

The whale-fishery is not more distinguished for examples of sudden peril and besetment than for unexpected deliverance from the most alarming situations.

"Three Dutch ships, after having completed a rich cargo on the northern coast of Spitzbergen, were at once so completely beset, that the crews in general urged the necessity of proceeding over the ice, and endeavoring to reach some other vessel. The captain of one of the three, however, strongly urged the obligation of doing all in their power to preserve such valuable property, and they agreed to make a further trial; when, in twenty days, the ice opened, and they had a happy voyage homeward.

The Dame Maria Elizabeth, had set out early for the fishery, and was so fortunate as, by the 30th of May, to have taken fourteen whales. Then, however, a violent gale from the south blew in the ice with such violence, that the captain found himself completely beset, and saw two Dutch vessels and one English go to pieces at a little distance. At length a brisk gale from the north gave him the hope of being extricated; when presently he was involved in a dense fog, which froze so thick upon the sails and rigging, that the ship appeared a mere floating iceberg. As the atmosphere cleared, the faint light, and the birds winging their way to the southward, announced the closing in of win-

ter. Unable to make any progress, the seamen looked forward in despair to the pros-
pect of spending the season in that frozen
latitude. They had nearly come to the end
of their provisions, and famine was already
staring them in the face, when they thought
of broiling the whales' tails, which proved
very eatable, and even salutary against the
scurvy. Thus they hoped to exist till the
middle of February, beyond which the pros-
pect was very dismal; but on the 12th No-
vember there arose a violent north wind,
which dispersed the ice. Their hopes being
now awakened, every effort was strained;
and on the 18th a north-wester brought on
so heavy a rain, that next day they were entirely clear of the ice, and had a prosperous
voyage homeward.

Capt. Broerties, in the Guillamine, arrived

on the 22d June at the great bank of northern ice, where he found fifty vessels moored and busied in the fishery. He began it prosperously : the very next day indeed he killed a large whale. The day after, a tempest drove in the ice with such violence that twenty-seven of the ships were beset, of which ten were lost. Broerties, on the 25th July, seeing some appearance of an opening, caused his ship to be warped through by the boats; but, after four days' labor, she found herself, with four other ships in a narrow basin, enclosed by icy barriers on every side.

On the 1st August the ice began to gather thick, and a violent storm driving it against the vessels, placed them in the greatest peril for a number of days. On the 20th a dreadful gale arose from the north-east, in which the Guillamine suffered very considerable damage. In this awful tempest, out of the five ships two went down, while a third had sprung a number of leaks. The crews were taken on board of the two remaining barks, which they greatly incommoded. On the 25th all the three were completely frozen in, when it was resolved to send a party of twelve men to seek aid from four vessels which a few days before had been driven into a station at a little distance; but by the time of their arrival two of these had been dashed to pieces, and the other two were in the most deplorable condition. Two Hamburgh ships, somewhat farther removed, had perished in a similar manner. Meantime the former came in sight of Gale Hamkes' Land, in Greenland, and the tempest still pushing them gradually to the southward, Iceland at length appeared on their left. The two more distant ships found a little opening, through which they contrived to escape. The crews of the three others were beginning to hope that they might at last be equally fortunate, when, on the 13th September, a whole mountain of ice fell upon the Guillamine. The men, half naked, leaped out upon the frozen surface, saving with difficulty a small portion of their provisions. The broken remnants of the vessel were soon buried under enormous piles of ice. Of the two other ships, one commanded by Jeldert Janz had just met a similar fate, and there remained only that of one other, to which all now looked for refuge. By leaping from one fragment of ice to another, the men, not without danger, contrived to reach this vessel, which, though in extreme distress, received them on board.   Shattered and overcrowded, she was obliged immediately after to accommodate fifty other seamen, the crew of a Hamburg ship which had just gone down, the chief harpooner and twelve of the mariners having perished.   These numerous companies, squeezed into one vessel, suffered every kind of distress.   Famine, in its most direful forms, began to stare them in the face.   All remoter fears, however, gave way, when on the 11th October, the vessel went to pieces in the same sudden manner as the others, leaving to the unfortunate sailors scarcely time enough to leap upon the ice with their remaining stores. With great difficulty they reached a field of some extent, and contrived with their torn sails to rear a sort of covering; but, sensible that, by remaining on this desolate spot, they must certainly perish, they saw no safety except in scrambling over the frozen surface to the coast of Greenland, which was in view. With infinite toil they effected their object, and happily met some inhabitants, who received them hospitably, and regaled them with dried fish and seals' flesh. Thence they pushed across that dreary region till they succeeded at length, on the 13th March, in reaching the Danish settlement of Frederickshaab. Here they were received with the utmost kindness, and, being recruited from their fatigues, took the first opportunity of embarking for Denmark, whence they afterward sailed to their native country.

The Davis's Strait fishery has also been marked with very frequent and fatal shipwrecks. In 1814 the Royalist, Capt. Edmonds, perished with all her crew; and in 1817, the London, Capt. Mathews, shared the same fate. The only account of either of these ships ever received was from Capt. Bennet of the Venerable, who, on the 15th April, saw the London in a tremendous storm, lying to windward of an extensive chain of icebergs, among which, it is probable she was dashed to pieces that very evening. Large contributions were raised at Hull for the widows and families of the seamen who had suffered on these melancholy occasions.

Among accidents on a smaller scale, one of the most frequent is, that of boats employed in pursuit of the whale being overtaken by deep fogs or storms of snow, which separate them from the ship, and never allow them to regain it. A fatal instance of

this kind occurred to the Ipswich, Capt.
Gordon; four of whose boats, after a whale
had been caught, and even brought to the
ship's side, were employed on a piece of ice
hauling in the line, when a storm suddenly
arose, caused the vessel to drift away, and
prevented her, notwithstanding the utmost
efforts, from ever coming within reach of the
unfortunate crews who composed the greater part of her establishment. Mr. Scoresby mentions several casualties of the same
nature which occurred to his boats' companies, all of whom, however, in the end, happily found their way back. One of the most
alarming cases was that of fourteen men who
were left on a small piece of floating ice,
with a boat wholly unable to withstand the
surrounding tempest; but amid their utmost
despair they fell in with the Lively of Whit-

by, and were most cordially received on board.

The source, however, of the most constant alarm to the whale-fisher is connected with the movements of that powerful animal, against which, with most unequal strength, he ventures to contend. Generally, indeed, the whale, notwithstanding his immense strength, is gentle, and even passive; seeking, even when he is most hotly pursued, to escape from his assailants, by plunging into the lowest depths of the ocean. Sometimes, however, he exerts his utmost force in violent and convulsive struggles; and every thing with which, when thus enraged, he comes into collision, is dissipated or destroyed in an instant. The Dutch writers mention Capt. Vienkes of the ship Barley Mill, who, after a whale had been struck, was hastening with a second boat to the support of the first. The fish, however, rose, and with its head struck the boat so furiously, that it was shivered to pieces, and Vienkes was thrown with its fragments on the back of the huge animal. Even then this bold mariner darted a second harpoon into the body of his victim; but unfortunately he got entangled in the line and could not extricate himself, while the other party were unable to approach near enough to save him. At last, however, the harpoon was disengaged, and he swam to the boat.

Mr. Scoresby, in one of his earliest voyages, saw a boat thrown several yards into the air, from which it fell on its side, plunging the crew into the sea. They were happily taken up, when only one was found to have received a severe contusion. Capt. Lyons of the Raith of Leith, on the Labrador coast, in 1802, had a boat thrown fifteen feet into the air; it came down into the water with its keel upwards, yet all the men except one were saved.

The crew of Mr. Scoresby the elder, in 1807, had struck a whale, which soon reappeared, but in a state of such violent agitation that no one durst approach it. The captain courageously undertook to encounter it in a boat by himself, and succeeded in striking a second harpoon; but another boat having advanced too close, the animal brandished its tail with so much fury, that the harpooner, who was directly under, judged it most prudent to leap into the sea. The tail then struck the very place that he had left, and cut the boat entirely asunder, with the exception of two planks, which were saved by having a coil of ropes laid over them; so that had he remained, he must have been dashed to pieces. Happily all the others escaped injury. The issues, however, were not always so fortunate. The Aimwell of Whitby in 1810, lost three men out of seven, and, in 1812, the Henrietta of the same port lost four out of six, by the boats being upset, and the crews thrown into the sea.

In 1809, one of the men belonging to the Resolution of Whitby, struck a sucking whale ; after which the mother, being seen wheeling rapidly round the spot, was eagerly watched. Mr. Scoresby, being on this occasion in the capacity of harpooner in another boat, was selecting a situation for the probable reappearance of the parent fish, when suddenly an invisible blow stove in fifteen feet of the bottom of his barge, which filled with water and instantly sank. The crew were saved.

CHAPTER V.

PROCEEDINGS AFTER A WHALE IS KILLED.

" Before a whale can be flensed, as the operation of taking off the fat and whalebone is called, some preliminary measures are requisite. These consist in securing the fish to a boat, cutting away the attached whale-lines, lashing the fins of the whale together, and towing it to the ship.

The first operation performed on a dead whale is to secure it to a boat. This is easily effected by lashing it with a rope, passed several times through two holes pierced in the tail, to the boat's bow. The more difficult operation of freeing the whale from the entanglement of the lines is then attempted. As the whale, when dead, always lies on its back, or on its side, the lines and harpoons are generally far under water. While this is in progress, the men of the other boats, having first lashed the tail to a boat, are employed in lashing the fins together across the belly of the whale.

On one occasion, says a whaler, I was engaged in the capture of a fish, upon which, when to appearance dead, I leaped, cut holes in the fins, and was in the act of reeving a rope through them, when the fish sunk beneath my feet. As soon as I observed that the water had risen above my knees, I made a spring towards a boat at the distance of three or four yards from me, and caught hold of the gunwale. Scarcely was I on board before the fish began to move forward, turned from its back upon its belly, reared its tail aloft and began to shake it with such prodigious violence, that it resounded through the air to the distance of two or three miles. After two or three minutes of this violent exercise, it ceased, rolled over upon its side, and died.

In the year 1816, a fish was to all appearance killed. The fins were partly lashed, and the tail on the point of being secured, and all the lines excepting one were cut away, the fish meanwhile lying as if dead. To the astonishment and alarm, however, of the sailors, it revived, began to move, and pressed forward in a convulsive agitation; soon after, it sunk in the water to some depth, and then died. One line remained attached to it, by which it was drawn up and secured. A fish being properly secured, is then "taken in tow," that is, all the boats join themselves in a line, by ropes always carried for the purpose, and unite their efforts in rowing towards the ship. The course of the ship, in the mean time, is directed towards the boats, but in calms, or when the ship is moored to the ice, at no great distance, or when the situation of the fish is inconvenient or inaccessible, the ship awaits the approach of the fish.

The fish having reached the ship is taken to the larboard side, arranged and secured for flensing. For the performance of this operation a variety of knives and other instruments is requisite.

The enormous weight of a whale prevents the possibility of raising it more than one fourth, or one fifth part out of the water, except, indeed, when it has been some days dead, in which case it swells in consequence of air generated by putrefaction, until one third of its bulk appears above the surface; the fish then lying belly upwards, extended and well secured, is ready for the operation of flensing.

After the whale is properly secured along side of the ship, the harpooners, having their feet armed with spurs, to prevent them from slipping, descend upon the fish. Two boats each of which is under the guidance of one or two boys, attend upon them, and serve to hold all their knives, and other apparatus. Thus provided, the harpooners divide the fat into oblong pieces, or 'slips,' by means of 'blubber spades' and 'blubber knives;' then, affixing a 'tackle' to each slip, flay it progressively off as it is drawn upwards. The flensers commence with the belly and under jaw, being the only part then above water. The blubber, in pieces of half a ton each, is received on deck, and divided into portable, cubical, or oblong pieces, containing near a solid foot of fat, and passed down between decks, when it is packed in a receptacle provided for it in the hold, or other suitable place, called the flens-gut, where it remains until further convenience.

All the fat being taken away from the belly, and the right fin removed, the fish is then turned round on its side. As the fish is turned round, every part of the blubber becomes successively uppermost and is removed. At length, when the whole of the blubber, whalebone, and jaw bones have been taken on board, the carcass being set at liberty, generally sinks in the water and disappears."

When sharks are present they generally

help themselves very plentifully during the cutting up. Birds pay close attendance, particularly the larger species of Petrel or Mother Cary's Chicken, seizing the pieces of flesh as it falls in the water. Gulls also attend in great numbers to get their share; but the large Petrel or Fulmar is decidedly master of the feast. Hence the others are obliged to relinquish the most delicious morsel when he claims it.

CREW OF A WHALER KILLING PENGUINS.

CATCHING SEAL ON THE ISLANDS OF THE PACIFIC.

HARP SEAL.

CHAPTER VI.

THE DIFFERENT SPECIES OF SEALS—THE FISHERY ON THE
ISLANDS OF THE PACIFIC, &c.

THERE are six different species of seal
sought after by man for their skins and fur,
viz. the Common Seal, which frequents the
sea-coasts throughout the world, the Hood-

ed Seal, the Great Seal, the Harp Seal, the
Fetid Seal, and the Ursine Seal. The five
last species are found on the shores of
Greenland. The Great Seal grows to the
size of ten or twelve feet; he is generally
found resting upon cakes of floating ice, and
resembles the Common Seal in his habits as
well as in his appearance, but is readily distinguished by its size and its large beard-
like whiskers. They are very timid, hence
the Greenlanders are seldom able to trap
them. The Esquimaux make ropes of the
skins of this species.

The Harp Seal is about eight feet long,
and is remarkable for its various colors.
When full grown it is of a greyish white color, having upon its back a black figure like
two half moons, in the form as represented
in the plate. It is quite common in the

Greenland seas, where it frequents the deep bays, migrating to and leaving them twice a year, going in March and returning in May, and again in June to return in September. At the breeding season they have but one young cub, which they nurse upon floating cakes of ice, at a great distance from the land. They live in great herds, swimming and playing together, apparently under the direction of an old one as a leader. They are seldom found upon the fixed ice, but seem to prefer the floating or drifting masses. The Greenlanders take them frequently by surrounding and pursuing them with loud noise whenever they come to the surface to breathe. Its skin is used by the Esquimaux to cover their tents and boats.

The Fetid Seal is about four and a half feet long; the hair on this seal is rough like

that of a pig; hence their skins are used by
the Greenlanders for clothing, the rough side
being generally turned inwards. This seal
frequents the ice near the land, seldom leaving its favorite haunts which are near holes
in the ice for the purpose of fishing; is soli-
tary in its habits, pairs being rarely seen together; and is not very timid, as the Northern eagle will occasionally pounce upon it
while asleep upon the surface. Their flesh
is not esteemed as food even by the voracious Esquimaux.

The last species of this genus, is the Ursine Seal, which is a large animal, being five
feet in circumference, and weighing from
eight to nine hundred pounds. They are
found on the islands which lie between
America and Kamtschatka, where they ar-
rive in the month of June and remain until

September, and are then very fat. They lie upon the shores in vast herds, but are separated into families, one large male being surrounded by fifteen or twenty females, which they seem to guard with great care. They are very quarrelsome, particularly the old males, and sometimes a large flock amounting to upwards of 100 individuals have furious battles upon the shore. They inflict very severe wounds upon each other during their combats, and when they cease to fight, plunge into the sea in order to wash off the blood with which they may be stained. The males are quite fond of their offspring, but cruelly tyrannical to the females. When any one attempts to catch one of their cubs, the male opposes the aggressor, while the female tries to secure the cub by carrying it off in her mouth; but should she un-

fortunately drop it, the male attacks her and
beats her dreadfully against the stones.
Capt. Foster says that the cubs are quite
fierce, and bark and bite at any one passing
them.   This seal is a very swift swimmer,
moving at the rate of seven or eight miles
an hour, and is able to remain under water a
much longer time than the Common Seal.

We now come, my son, to the Common
Seal, which is found not only throughout the
northern seas of both continents, but upon
our own shores, and is the seal which furnishes the inhabitants of those cold and fri-
gid climes with nearly all their necessaries
and luxuries.   What a striking display of
the goodness of the all-wise Creator do we
find in giving to the Esquimaux, who are de-
nied the opportunity of deriving their sub-
sistence from animals which depend upon

the vegetable kingdom for nutriment, the abundance of seals, supplying to them the place of flocks and herds, without requiring from those fed and clothed by them any provision for their maintenance. The manner in which the seal feeds is very interesting : when fish are thrown into a tub where several of these animals may be together, they eagerly spring to a considerable distance in the air, raising half their bodies out of the water and stretching out their necks to the utmost. If the fish is caught by the tail, it it is then turned head foremost and swallowed whole. They also feed under water and swallow with as much ease as in the air, but in a different manner, which is to open its mouth partially.

Seals are animals of passage ; when on their travels or migrations, vast droves are

5

seen moving along through the openings of
the ice, swimming with their heads always
out of the water. They are very timid, seldom sleeping above five minutes at a time.
Three of the common seal were taken a few
years since on our coast in a net; they
fought desperately and were with great difficulty secured. After a few months, however, they became very tame, and one of them
was taught to perform many tricks, placing
himself in different attitudes at the com-
mand of his keeper. They all died during
the winter.

There were two young seals kept in a
museum at Paris, which showed no fear in
the presence of men or other animals, never
attempting to escape or withdraw themselves, unless to avoid being trodden on, and
then merely removing to a short distance.

One of them would occasionally threaten
with its voice and strike with its paw, but
would never bite unless extremely provo-
ked. They were very voracious, yet showed no ill temper when their food was taken
from them, and some young dogs, to which
one of the seals was attached, would snatch
the fish from his mouth just as he was about
to swallow it, without the seal showing any
sign of anger. When both the seals were
suffered to eat together, they usually fought
with their paws, and the strongest drove the
other away.

One of these seals was at first very shy,
and retreated when any one attempted to
caress him, yet in a few days he became
quite tame and confident of the kindness of
those who approached him. When shut up
with two little dogs that used to mount up-

on his back and playfully bark and bite at
him, he soon entered into the spirit of their
actions, and took pleasure in their frolics,
striking them gently with his paw rather to
encourage than repress them. When the
dogs ran off he would follow them, though
the ground was covered with stones and
mud. During cold weather he would lie in
close company with the dogs for the sake of
their mutual warmth. The other seal evinced a strong degree of attachment to the
keeper, recognizing him at a considerable
distance, and using many expressive ges-
tures and looks to solicit his attention and
obtain food, the idea of which was no doubt
associated with the presence of the keeper.
These seals barked commonly in the evening, or on a change of weather, though with
a much feebler voice than that of the dog;

their anger was exhibited by a kind of hissing noise. A young seal, which was given by the master of a whaler to the officers of the Alexander, one of the ships on the former voyage, became so entirely domesticated and attached to the ship that it was frequently put into the sea and suffered to swim at perfect liberty, and when tired would return of itself to the boats and be taken in.

The common seal brings forth two young in autumn, and suckles them on shore until they are six or seven weeks old, when they are gradually accustomed by their parents to frequent the sea. At this period they are generally of a whitish or light fawn color, covered with soft or woolly hair, and when in distress or hurt have a sort of whining voice. Seals are mostly associated in families consisting of a few males and a large

number of females and young ones. They
are fond of landing on the sea-beach, ledges
of rocks or ice-banks, for the purpose of bask-
ing in the sun, and in fine weather prefer
being on the ice to remaining in the water;
sometimes indeed they are very averse to
take to the water when they have been out
of it long enough to become perfectly dry.

When on their passage from one place to
another they swim in very large flocks or
shoals, and become visible to the mariner
every few minutes, as they are obliged to
come to the surface to breathe; this is generally done by the whole company nearly at
the same time, when they spring up so as to
raise their heads, necks, and even their
whole bodies, out of the water. From the
peculiar vivacity of their movements and
general sportiveness of the company, such

a shoal of these animals has obtained from the sailors the designation of a " seal's wedding."

The seal is peculiarly vigilant, and whenever a herd of them visit the shore some are always on the look out, and a seal when alone is observed very frequently to raise its head for the purpose of discovering the approach of enemies.

Seals are sometimes enticed to the surface by music, or the whistling of an individual who is prepared to shoot them, and this proves that they can hear far better when under water than we might be inclined to believe from a mere glance at their external ears. When they hear this sound they come to the surface, elongate their necks to the utmost extent, and expose them fully to the aim of the hunter. They are most

effectually secured however by firing duck
or other shot, which blinds them, so that
they may be approached and despatched;
when killed at once by a single bullet they
most commonly sink.   Another mode of
killing the seal is to go to the caves on shore,
into which herds of seals occasionally enter.
When the sealers are properly placed they
raise a simultaneous shout, at which the af-
frighted animals rush out in great confusion,
and are despatched with wonderful quick-
ness by a single blow on the nose, struck
with a club.   They are very tenacious of
life when struck or wounded on any other
part of the body.

Where the seals are very numerous the
sealers stop not to flay those they have killed, but set off to another ice-field to kill
more, merely leaving one man behind to take

GREENLAND SEAL HUNTING.

off the skins and fat. When the condition of the ice forbids the use of boats, the hunter is obliged to pursue the seals over it, jumping from piece to piece, until he succeeds in taking one, which he then stops to flay and flense, or to remove the skin and fat. This sometimes is horrible business, since many of the seals are merely stunned, and occasionally recover after they have been flayed and flensed. In this condition, too shockingly mangled for description, they have been seen to make battle, and even to swim off.

The Esquimaux hunt the seal in various modes, according to circumstances. When the breathing place (a hole made in the ice by the seal) is discovered, the hunter raises near it a small wall about four feet high, of slabs of snow, to shelter himself from the wind, and sits under the lee of his snow shelter, having deposited his spear, lines and other implements upon several little forked sticks set up in the snow, in order to avoid making the slightest noise in moving them when wanted. The most curious precaution, taken with a similar intention, is that of tying his own knees together with a thong to prevent any rustling of his dress, which would alarm the seal. In this situation the Esquimaux will frequently sit for many hours when the thermometer is below zero, attentively listening to ascertain whether the animal is working below.

When he thinks the hole is almost completed, he carefully raises his spear, to which the line is previously tied, and the moment the breathing of the seal is distinctly heard, the ice being then of course very thin, he strikes the spear into him with both hands, and cuts away the ice with his knife to repeat his blow. At other times, having enlarged the breathing place, he takes his position behind the shelter, and the animal, when he next comes to the hole, rises fearlessly out of the water, exposing his head and shoulders, and repeats this action with increased confidence. As he is not in haste to dive again, the hunter now starts up suddenly and drives his spear forcibly into him. Another method adopted consists in covering the breathing hole with light snow, and making an opening through the top of it with the spear handle about as large as the mouth of a bottle. The hunter then withdraws the spear and takes his place behind his snow-screen, listening vigilantly until he hears the seal breathing beneath the snow, when he silently rises and plunges his weapon through the snow-covering into the body of the seal. The moment the seal is struck, the hunter endeavors to catch the line behind one leg to act as a strong check; and as an additional security, a hitch is taken round the ring finger, which is sometimes either dreadfully lacerated or entirely torn off by the violent struggles of a large seal. The animal is then stabbed until dead; the hole being enlarged, it is drawn out on the ice, where it speedily freezes and is in condition to be drawn home.

I have told you, my son, that the seal furnishes the natives of those cold climates with nearly all the necessaries of life, and I will now give you a description of Capt. Lyon's visit to one of their feasts.

" On the return of a party of successful

seal-hunters, he says, " blood, blubber, entrails, skins and flesh, was sociably intermix-
ed in savoury heaps. Abundant smoking
messes were in preparation, and even the
dogs looked happy as they uninterruptedly
licked the faces of the children, who were
covered with blood and grease from the chin
to the eyes. Universal merriment prevail-
ed, and such men and children as could bear
more food stood lounging round the women,
who sat sucking their fingers and cooking
as fast as possible. While the messes were
preparing the children solaced themselves
by eating such parts of the raw uncleaned
entrails as their young teeth could tear, and
those morsels which proved too tough were
delivered over to their mothers, who soon
reduced them to a proper size and consis-
tency for their tender offspring.

"At the distribution of the contents of one of the pots I was complimented with a fine piece of half stewed seal's flesh, from which the kind donor, a most unsavory looking old lady, with the most obliging politeness, had first licked the gravy and dirt, and bitten it all round in order to ascertain the most tender part on which I should make the first attack. My refusal of this delicacy did not offend, and we had much laughing on the subject, particularly when the old woman, with well feigned disgust and many wry faces, contrived to finish it herself. In my rambles on this day of plenty I found, beyond a doubt, that the women do not eat with the men, but waiting till they are first satisfied, then enjoy a feast by themselves. In the meantime, however, the females who superintend the cooking have the privilege

of licking the gravy from the lumps of meat
as they are taken out and before they are
presented to their husbands. Both sexes
eat in the same manner, although not in
equal proportions; the females very seldom,
and the men very frequently stuffing until
they become quite stupified. A lump of
meat being given to the nearest person, he
first sucks it all round and then pushes as
much as he can into his mouth, cutting it
from the larger piece close to his lips, to the
great danger of them and his nose. The
meat then passes round until it is consumed,
and the person before whom it stops is enti-
tled to the first bite of the next morsel. In
this manner a meal continues a long time, as
each eats or rather bolts several pounds, and
the pots are in consequence frequently re-
plenished. In the intermediate time the

6

convives suck their fingers or indulge in a
few lumps of delicate raw blubber. The
swallows of the Esquimaux are of such a
marvellous capacity that a piece of flesh of
the size of an orange very rarely receives
half a dozen bites before it is bolted, and
that without any apparent exertion. The
rich soup of the meat is handed round
at the close of the repast, and each takes a
sup in turn until it is finished, when the pot
is passed to the good woman of the house,
who licks it carefully clean and then pre-
pares to make a mess for herself. On all occasions the children are stuffed almost to
suffocation. The meals being finished, every one scrapes the grease, &c. from his face
into his mouth, and the fingers are then
cleaned by sucking."

The food of the Esquimaux is cooked by

the aid of a lamp, which is supplied with
seal oil, the wick being composed of moss.
On this lamp are they also dependent for
warmth in their huts, which are made of
snow, as well as for their supply of water to
drink, which, during a great part of the year
is only to be obtained by melting snow. A
scarcity of seals, therefore, is accompanied
by a series of ills, the hut is deprived of light
and warmth, and the sufferings of famine
are increased by the torment of thirst,
against which they have no other resource
under such circumstances except to eat the
snow, which affords but a partial relief. In
judging of the filth and voracity of these poor
creatures, we must ever bear in mind the
circumstances which during so much of the
time render water almost unattainable, except to quench their thirst, as well as the fre-

quent and severe starvation to which they are subjected.

The Esquimaux apply the skins of seals to various purposes, amongst which the most important is the construction of their boats. The small boat to carry but one person is called *kayak*, and has been aptly compared in shape to a weaver's shuttle, having the head and stern equally sharp. There is an opening or hole in which the rower sits, having a rim or projection to which a part of the dress may be fastened in such a manner as entirely to exclude the water. The weight of the whole does not exceed fifty or sixty pounds, so that the boat may be readily carried by the owner on his head, and from the peculiar form of the rim, without applying his hands.

The Esquimaux are very proud of their

boats; they place a warm skin in the bottom to sit upon, and the position of the paddler is with the legs extended and the feet pointed forwards. Whenever any weight is to be raised, or the stowage of the boat to be changed, two kayaks lie together, and the paddles of each being laid across, a steady double boat is formed. When not paddling the occupant must preserve a very nice balance, and a tremulous motion is always to be observed in the boat. The Esquimaux in the vicinity of Winter Island have not the art of regaining the upright position when overturned by a dexterous use of the paddle. An inflated seal bladder is a constant appendage to the canoe equipage; the weapons are kept in their places on the upper surface of the boats by small lines of whalebone, tightly stretched across so as to receive the points or handles of the spears beneath them. The stem or stern of the boat is frequently stowed with flesh, birds or eggs; a seal, notwithstanding its roundness and liability to roll, is so carefully balanced on the boat as seldom to require being tied on. When going before the wind while a smart swell is running, the kayak requires the nicest management, as the slightest inattention would expose the broadside to the sea and be followed by immediate peril to this frail vessel. The extreme velocity with which the kayak is impelled, and the dexterity with which it is turned and guided, render it a very interesting object.

The Esquimaux use another boat made of seal-skin, which is larger and destined to carry luggage, or to transport their families. This is called *umiak* or *oomiak*, and is made

nearly square at the head and stern. Its
frame is made of whale-bone or wood, and
the bottom is flat. The seal skins with
which the frame is covered are deprived of
the hair, and are at all times transparent,
but especially so when wet. Each of the
boats has five or six seats or thwarts, placed
as in ours, and is moved by two very clumsy
oars with flat blades, which are used by the
women, and steered with a similar oar by
another. They vary much in size, having
the sides very flat and about three feet high.
Sometimes they are so large as twenty-five
feet in length by eight in breadth, and are
capable of containing women, boys and small
children, to the number of twenty-one persons.

As I have alluded to the Esquimaux, my
son, it will perhaps be interesting to you to

hear something further of their mode of life. I will therefore give you a description of one of their snow villages, with an account of a visit by a large party of them to the winter quarters of captains Parry and Lyon, which is taken from the Narrative of Discovery and Adventure in the Polar Seas and Regions.

"On the morning of the 1st February, a number of distant figures were seen moving over the ice, and, when they were viewed through glasses, the cry was raised, ' Esquimaux ! Esquimaux !' As it was of great importance to deal courteously and discreetly with these strangers, the two commanders formed a party of six, who walked in files behind each other, that they might cause no alarm. The Esquimaux then formed themselves into a line of twenty-one, advanced slowly, and at length made a full stop. In this order they saluted the strangers by the usual movement of beating their breasts. They were substantially clothed in rich and dark deer-skins, and appeared a much more quiet and orderly race than their rude countrymen of the Savage Islands. On the English producing their precious commodities, knives, nails, and needles, an active traffic was set on foot; and the females, on seeing that much importance was attached to the skins which formed their clothing, began immediately to strip off those with which their fair persons were covered. The captains felt alarm for the consequences, under a temperature more than fifty degrees below the freezing point; but were soon consoled by discerning underneath another comfortable suit. They were now cordially invited to enter their habitations, to which they agreed most readily, only that there appeared no habitations to enter. However, they were led to a hole in the snow, and instructed to place themselves on their hands and knees, in which position, having crept through a long winding passage, they arrived at a little hall with a dome-shaped roof, whence doors opened into three apartments, each occupied by a separate family. These proved to be five distinct mansions, tenanted by sixty-four men, women, and children. The materials and structure of these abodes were still more singular than their position. Snow, the chief product of the northern tempests, became here a protection against its own cold. It was formed into curved slabs of about two feet long and half a foot thick, put together by a most judicious masonry, so as to present a species of dome-shaped structures, rising six or seven feet above the ground, and about fourteen or sixteen feet in diameter. The mode of inserting the key-slab, which bound the whole together, would, it is said, have been satisfactory to the eye of a regularly-bred artist. A plate of ice in the roof served as a window, and admitted the light as through ground glass; which, when it shone on the interior mansions, in their first state of pure and beautiful transparency, produced soft and glittering tints of green and blue. But, alas! ere long, accumulated dirt, smoke, and offal, converted these apartments into a scene of blackness and stench. This little village appeared at first like a cluster of hillocks amid the snow; but successive falls filled up the vacuities, and converted it almost into a smooth

surface, so that even boys and dogs were
seen walking and sporting over the roofs;
though, as summer and thaw advanced, a leg
sometimes penetrated, and appeared to the
alarmed inmates below.   Then, too, the ceil-
ing begins to drip; and the tenants, after re-
peatedly endeavoring to patch it with fresh
slabs, and catching, of course, some severe
colds, are obliged to betake themselves to a
more durable covering.   In each room, sus-
pended from the roof, burns a lamp, with a
long wick formed of a peculiar species of
moss, fed with the oil of the seal or the wal-
rus, and serving at once for light, heat and
cookery.   The family sit round the apart-
ment, on a bench formed of snow, strewed
with slender twigs and covered with skins;
but this part of the dwelling must be carefully kept a good deal below the freezing-

point, since a higher temperature would speedily dissolve the walls of the frail tenement.

After a cheerful and friendly visit, an invitation was given to the Esquimaux to repair to the ships, when fifty accepted it with alacrity. Partly walking, and partly dancing, they soon reached the vessels, where a striking congeniality of spirit was soon found to exist between them and the sailors; boisterous fun forming to each the chief source of enjoyment. A fiddle and drum being produced, the natives struck up a dance, or rather a succession of vehement leaps, accompanied with loud shouts and yells. Seeing the Kabloonas or Whites, as they called the strangers, engaged in the game of leap-frog, they attempted to join; but not duly understanding how to measure their move-

ments, they made such over-leaps as sometimes to pitch on the crown of their heads:
however they sprang up quite unconcerned.
Their attention was specially attracted to
the effects of a winch, by which one sailor
forcibly drew towards him a party of ten or
twelve of their number, though grinning and
straining every nerve in resistance; but find-
ing all in vain, they joined in the burst of
good-humored laughter till tears streamed
from their eyes. One intelligent old man
followed captain Lyon to the cabin, and
viewed with rational surprise various ob-
jects which were presented. The performance of a hand-organ and a musical snuff-
box struck him with breathless admiration;
and on seeing drawings of the Esquimaux
in Hudson's Strait, he soon understood them,
and showed the difference between their

dress and appearance and that of his own tribe. On seeing the sketch of a bear, he raised a loud cry, drew up his sleeves, and showed the scars of three deep wounds received in encounters with that terrible animal. The seamen sought to treat their visitors to such delicacies as their ship afforded, but were for some time at a loss to discover how their palate might be gratified. Grog, the seaman's choicest luxury, only one old woman could be induced to taste. Sugar, sweetmeats, gingerbread, were accepted only out of complaisance, and eaten with manifest disgust; but train-oil, entrails of animals, and any thing consisting of pure fat or grease, were swallowed in immense quantities, and with symptoms of exquisite delight. This taste was first evinced by an old woman, who, having sold her oil-pot,

took care previously to empty the contents
into her stomach, and lick it clean with her
tongue, regardless of her face becoming thus
as black as soot. Capt. Lyon, being dispo-
sed to ingratiate himself with rather a hand-
some young damsel, presented her with a
good moulded candle, six in the pound. She
immediately began to eat off the tallow with
every symptom of the greatest enjoyment,
after which she thrust the wick into her
mouth ; but the captain, concerned for the
consequences to this delicate virgin, insist-
ed on pulling it out.   In preference to
strong liquors they drank water in the most
enormous quantities, by gallons at a time,
and two quarts at a draught; a supply of li-
quid which is perhaps necessary to dissolve
their gross food, and which, being obtained
only from snow artificially melted, is a scarce
winter article.

The Esquimaux were attended by a large pack of wolves, which seemed to follow solely to pick up whatever might be found straggling or defenceless about their habitation. These animals continued through the whole winter ravening with hunger, and in eager watch for any victim which might come within their reach. For this purpose they took a station between the huts and the ships, ready to act against either as circumstances might dictate. They did not attack the sailors even when unarmed, though they were often seen hovering through the gloom in search of prey. Every stray dog was seized, and in a few minutes devoured. Two wolves broke into a snow-house close to the ship, and carried off each a dog larger than himself; but, being pursued, one of them was obliged to drop his booty. In the

7

extremity of their hunger they hesitated not
to tear and devour the cables and canvass
found lying near the vessel. A deadly war
was therefore waged against these fierce animals, of which thirteen were killed in the
course of the season, and sent to be eaten
by the Esquimaux,—a present which was
received with much satisfaction."

The number of seals destroyed in a single
season by the regular sealers may well ex-
cite surprise; one ship has been known to
obtain a cargo of four or five thousand skins
and upwards of a hundred tons of oil.
Whale ships have accidentally fallen in with
and secured two or three thousand of these
animals during the month of April. The
sealing business is, however, very hazardous
when conducted on the borders of the Spitzbergen ice. Many ships with all their crews

are lost by the sudden and tremendous storms occurring in those seas, where the dangers are vastly multiplied by the driving of immense bodies of ice. In one storm that occurred in the year 1774 no less than five seal ships were destroyed in a few hours, and six hundred valuable seamen perished.

" One of the most affecting shipwrecks which ever occurred in the northern seas was that of the Jean, of Peterhead, in 1826. Of this we can give a full account from an interesting narrative by Mr. Cumming, the surgeon, an eye-witness and sharer of the calamity. This vessel sailed on the 15th March, having on board only twenty-eight men, but received at Lerwick a complement of twenty-three natives of Shetland; owing to which arrangement, as well as by contrary winds, she was detained till the 28th.

From the evening of that day to the 1st
April, the ship encountered very stormy
weather, which she successfully withstood,
and was then steered into those western
tracts of the Greenland sea which are the
most favorable for the capture of the seal.
In one day the seamen killed 1138 seals, and
the entire number caught in five days exceed-
ed 3070. This scene, however, could not
be contemplated without some painful im-
pressions. The seals attacked were only
the young, as they lay fearlessly reposing
on the ice, before they had yet attempted to
plunge into the watery element. One blow
of the club stunned them completely. The
view of hundreds of creatures bearing some
resemblance to the human form, writhing in
the agonies of death, and the deck stream-
ing with their gore, was at once distressing

and disgusting to a spectator of any feeling. However, this evil soon gave way to others of a more serious nature.

On the morning of the 18th April the sailors had begun their fishery as usual; but a breeze sprung up, and obliged them by eleven o'clock to suspend operations. The gale continually freshened, and was the more unpleasant from their being surrounded with loose ice, which a dense and heavy fog made it impossible to distinguish at any distance. The mariners took in all sail, but did not apprehend danger till six in the evening, when the wind, which had been continually increasing, began to blow with tenfold fury. All that the narrator had ever heard, of the united sounds of thunder, tempest, and waves, seemed faint when compared with the stunning roar of this hurricane. At eight the ship was borne upon a stream of ice, from which she received several severe concussions; the consequence of which was that at ten the water began to enter, and at twelve no exertion in pumping could prevent her from being gradually filled.

At one in the morning she became completely waterlogged. She then fell over on her beam-ends, when the crew, giving themselves up for lost, clung to the nearest object for immediate safety. By judiciously cutting away the main and fore masts, they happily enabled the ship to right herself, when being drifted into a stream of ice, she was no longer in danger of immediate sinking. The whole hull, however, was inundated and indeed immersed in water, except a portion of the quarter-deck, upon which the whole crew were now assembled. Here they threw up an awning of sails to shelter themselves from the cold, which had become so intense as to threaten the extinction of life. Those endowed with spirit and sense kept up the vital power by brisk movement; but the natives of Shetland, who are accused on such occasions of sinking into a selfish despondency, piled themselves together in a heap, with the view of deriving warmth from each other's bodies. Those in the interior of the mass obtained thus a considerable temperature, though accompanied with severe pressure; and blows were given, and even knives drawn to gain and to preserve this advantageous position. On the 19th, one Shetlander died of cold, another on the 20th, and a third on the 21st,—events felt by the others as peculiarly gloomy, chiefly, it is owned, as forming a presage of their own impending fate.

On the 22d the sun began to appear amid showers of snow; and the 23d was ushered in by fine weather and a clear sky. The opinions of the crew were now divided as to what course they should steer in search of deliverance. Two plans were suggested. They could either stretch northward into the fishing stations, where they might expect, sooner or later, to meet some of their countrymen, by whom they would be received on board; or they might sail southward towards Iceland, and throw themselves on the hospitality of its inhabitants. The former plan was in several respects the more promising, especially as a vessel had been in sight when the storm arose. But its uncertainties were also very great. They might traverse for weeks those vast icy seas, amid cold always increasing, and with imminent danger of being swallowed up by the waves. Iceland was distant, but it was a definite point; and upon this course they at last wisely determined. Several days were spent in fitting out their two remaining boats, all the others having been swept away—and in fishing up from the interior of the vessel every article which could be turned to account. During this operation, the weather continuing fine, they could not forbear admiring the scene by which they were surrounded. The sea was formed as it were into a beautiful little frith, by the ice rising around in the most varied and fantastic forms, sometimes even assuming the appearance of cities adorned with towers and forests of columns. Continual efforts were necessary, meantime, to keep the wreck on the icy field; for had it slipped over into the

sea, of which there appeared a strong pro-
bability, it would have gone down at once.
By the 26th the boats were completely ready, having on board a small stock of provisions, and a single change of linen.   At half
past one in the morning of the 27th, the mariners took leave, with some sorrow, of the
vessel, which ' seemed a home even in ruins,'
leaving the deck strewed with clothes, books,
and provisions, to be swallowed up by the
ocean as soon as the icy floor on which it
rested should melt away.

The two boats, having received forty-
seven men on board, lay very deep in the
water; so that when a smart breeze arose,
the men were obliged to throw away their
spare clothing and every thing else which
could be wanted, and soon saw their little
wardrobe floating on the face of the sea.

The seamen were frequently obliged to drag their boats over large fields of ice, and again to launch them. However, a favorable wind in ten hours enabled them to make forty-one miles, when they came to the utmost verge of the icy stream, and entered upon the open ocean. Their fears were not yet removed; for if a heavy gale had arisen, their slender barks must soon have been overwhelmed. There blew in fact a stiff breeze, which threw in a good deal of water, and caused severe cold; however, at seven in the evening, they saw, with inexpressible pleasure, the lofty and snow-capped mountains of Iceland. But these were still fifty miles off, and much might intervene; so that the night, which soon closed in, passed with a mixture of joy and fear. Fortunately the morning was favorable; and about four they saw a black speck on the surface of the ocean. It proved to be an island, naked, rocky, and seemingly uninhabited. On turning a promontory, however, what was their joy to see a boat pushing out to meet them! and they were received by the natives with every mark of kindness and compassion. The seamen were distributed among the half-subterraneous abodes, and received a portion of the frugal and scanty fare on which the inhabitants subsisted. After recruiting their strength, they set sail for the coast of Iceland, and after a tedious voyage, reached Akureyri, the capital of this quarter of the island. They were here also received with the most humane hospitality, and remained three months before they could obtain a passage home; during which delay unfortunately they lost nine of their number, chiefly from mortification and other morbid affections occasioned by extreme cold. In the middle of July, they procured a passage in a Danish vessel, which brought them and their boats near to the coast of Shetland. Having landed at Lerwick, they were conveyed by his Majesty's ship Investigator to Peterhead, where they arrived on the 5th August."

The Harp Seal, my son, of which you have a drawing upon the cover, is quite common in the Greenland seas, and shows much of the frisky or frolicksome disposition of the Common Seal. It is often seen gamboling and whirling over as if in play with its comrades. They live in great herds or companies, appearing to be under the direction of a leader, who watches over the safety of the whole. The Esquimaux and Greenlanders often drive them on shore, when

they come up to the surface in shallow water to breathe. The skin of this species
they use to cover their tents and boats.

Seal oil when properly prepared is pure
and fine, and may be employed for all purposes to which whale oil is adapted. The
skins of these animals are extensively consumed in various manufactures, especially
in trunk making, saddlery, &c.

And now, my son, do you not think that
the station in which a kind Providence has
allotted to you, there are not many, very
many reasons not only for contentment, but
gratitude to your heavenly Father for the
inestimable blessings conferred upon you.
How necessitous are the poor Esquimaux!
Their climate forbids their attempting the
gratification of any desires beyond the com-
monest animal wants. In the short summers

they hunt the reindeer; and during their long cold winters, the seal. But the most affecting circumstance to the Christian is their present condition in the scale of humanity, their deprivation of the means of knowledge, above all the knowledge of the Bible.

> " Weep, weep for the people that dwell
> Where the light of the truth never shone,
> Where anthems of praise never swell,
> And the love of the Lamb is unknown."

As you gain more knowledge of the different beings and things which God has made, you will gain also more and more proofs of his existence and of his amazing power, wisdom and goodness. Let that goodness sink deep into your soul, and form a part of your daily thoughts and feelings. How much kindness God has shown and is still showing you; how many sources of comfort and of enjoyment he gives you; how it grieves him to see you think or feel or act wrong; how he loves to see you be good and to do good, that you may go, after death, to be with him forever,— *continually to improve in knowledge, in holiness, and in happiness !*

Visit us at
www.historypress.net